THE ^{New} COMPLETE BOOK OF
CHICKEN WINGS

THE New COMPLETE BOOK OF CHICKEN WINGS

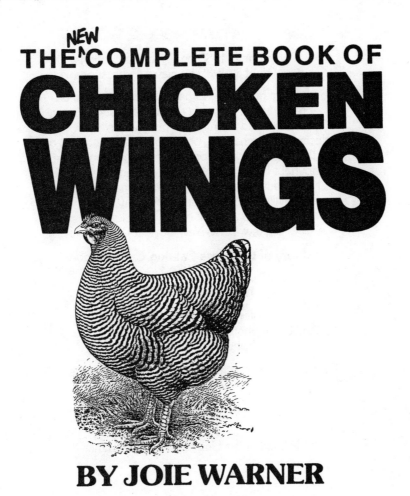

BY JOIE WARNER

HEARST BOOKS

New York

A FLAVOR BOOK

Copyright © 1985 by Flavor Publications
Copyright © 1989 by Flavor Publications

**Library of Congress Catalog Card Number:
85-60363**

ISBN: 0-688-05713-6

Photography by Ken Mulveney
Additional photography, page 10 and author's
photo: Drew Warner

This book was created, designed, and produced by
Flavor Publications, Inc.
208 East 51st Street, Suite 240
New York, New York 10022

Printed in the United States of America

4 5 6 7 8 9 10

Acknowledgments

I wish to thank my family and friends for their enthusiasm and encouragement during the creation of both the first and second edition of this book. My warmest thanks to Drew, as always, for his design and production expertise and for taste-testing even more wings! To my mother, Dorothy McPhee — my biggest promoter and still the most creative cook I know. I also wish to thank Connie and John Langley, Ken Mulveney, Judy and Dr. Leonard Katz, Joan Nagy, Frances Hanna, Alison Fryer, Kristina Goodwin, and the many wing lovers across North America who took the time to write to me. A very special thanks to Andy Ambraziejus of William Morrow for his unlimited patience and continuing enthusiasm for the book. And of course to the Bellissimo family of the Anchor Bar and to the City of Buffalo for creating and celebrating the classic Buffalo-Style Chicken Wings!

Contents

Introduction

If ever there was a perfect food for contemporary cooks — fun to make and a delight to eat — it is chicken wings. This remarkably adaptable cut of chicken responds well to a myriad of spices, seasonings, and marinades. What's more, wings are versatile: they can be broiled, barbecued, pan-fried, stir-fried, deep-fried, steamed, smoked, baked, and boned and stuffed. Terrific as main dishes, perfect for picnics, and superb as hors d'oeuvre, it is no wonder that wings have become enormously popular. People everywhere are devouring these toothsome delicacies in restaurants and bars and at backyard barbecues.

And why not? A meal of wings is undeniably a fun and casual event (it is utterly impossible to be formal and mannerly while eating with your fingers). They are a delicious break from trendy food and haute cuisine. In short, wings are relished by everyone — adults and kids alike.

There is no trick to cooking wings at home. They are exceedingly easy to prepare and guarantee raves for the cook. Moreover, they are a fabulous food bargain, low in calories, and ideal for no-fuss, laid-back entertaining with family and friends.

Although chicken wings have been enjoyed for centuries by many cultures — in particular the Chinese — it was not until 20 years ago that a funky Buffalo, New York, tavern began a major North

American food sensation by deep-frying some humble chicken wings, pouring a buttery hot sauce over them, and accompanying them with a side order of celery sticks and blue cheese dressing.

There are at least two restaurants that lay claim to the creation of the Buffalo wing phenomenon. John Young of John Young's Wings 'n Things insists he invented them and the Bellissimo family (namely, the founder of the Anchor Bar, the late Frank Bellissimo, his wife Teressa, and their son Dom) claim they are the inventors. This small controversy over who really did invent the fiery-sauced wings still rages, but the Anchor Bar has been officially proclaimed the originator of Buffalo chicken wings by the City of Buffalo. It says so on the back of their menu!

Food sleuth Calvin Trillin decided to find out for himself and in his book, *Third Helpings,* describes in rich detail how the actual moment came about.

Apparently one story is that Frank Bellissimo got a delivery to his restaurant of chicken wings instead of the backs and necks he ordered to make spaghetti sauce. So he asked his wife to do something special with them rather than just putting the wings into the sauce. Obviously inspired, Teressa proceeded to make a snack for the bar using some available ingredients — butter and hot sauce. After cutting off the wing tips and slicing the wings in half, she deep-fried them and immediately tossed them about in the buttery hot sauce. Teressa then found some celery sticks and some blue cheese

dressing, probably from the house salad, and served these alongside the wings. The Anchor Bar patrons were not quite sure which to dip in the dressing — the celery or the wings — but they were an enormous success nonetheless, and history was in the making.

Today Buffalo Style Wings (also known as New York Style Wings), or close facsimiles thereof are available in eating and drinking establishments all across North America. (In Buffalo alone, over 13½ tons of wings are served a month!) They have found their way to the South, the West Coast, and across the border to Canada. They have infiltrated Toronto, Buffalo's sister city to the north, at an astounding rate, with signs everywhere proclaiming "wing-nite," "all-you-can-eat wings," "Tuesday night is wingding night," and so on. Walk around your neighborhood as I did recently and check out the local eateries and you are likely to discover chicken wings on quite a few menus.

The great debate, it seems, among wing cognoscenti is which restaurant where serves the most authentic and delicious rendering. And at every informal "wingding" I have been to, the inevitable question is: Where does one find good chicken wing recipes?

In view of the popularity of wings and the difficulty in finding recipes, it occurred to me that a cookbook devoted to them was timely indeed because homemade chicken wings are vastly superior to restaurant wings. Thus the first and only chicken wing cookbook was born!

9

My book, I decided, should include mouth-watering (nothing less would do) recipes for wings and all the fixin's drawn from the great cuisines of the world. More than a year of compiling, researching, testing, and retesting has resulted in more than 70 outstanding recipes to savor, such as Famous Buffalo Style Wings, Black Bean Sauce Wings, scrumptious Parmesan Dijon Wings, Honey Curry Wings, Mexican Mole Sauce Wings, Soy Orange Wings, Hot Red Pepper Garlic Wings, exotic Tea Smoked Wings, and much, much more — all the classics plus many

Where it all began: The Anchor Bar, Buffalo, New York

original recipes.

I have also included delicious salads to serve alongside, plus side orders and dipping sauces to complete the repast.

In addition, you will find practical information on buying, storing, trimming, boning, and stuffing — even proper eating etiquette (which is basically to forget etiquette, dig in, and enjoy).

Wings may generally be thought of as humble fare, but with more and more North Americans choosing to entertain informally, this collection of delightfully different chicken wing recipes, along with everyone's popular favorites, will gratify both the accomplished and the novice cook and their family and friends, whatever the occasion.

Every recipe in the book is straightforward and quick to cook, perfect for the harried housewife or career person. In most cases, all you need are a few marinade ingredients poured over wings, which are then left for a couple of hours to marinate, placed on a broiling rack or barbecue, and cooked for approximately 15 to 20 minutes. Presto — nothing could be simpler and more delicious. Add a salad, a side order, icy cold beer, or wine and you have created an ambrosial feast.

There is no mystique to preparing good wings; only the most rudimentary skills are needed to prepare them. Actually it is quite difficult to cook up an unappetizing meal of them — unless of course you forget them in the oven and burn the wings to a crisp.

In fact, cooking wings is so staggeringly simple that I usually prepare two or three different recipes at the same time (one or two broiled, the other stir-fried or deep-fried, for example) for a truly memorable taste experience.

Only the most basic equipment is needed, and ingredients for the most part are easily found in supermarkets. Only a few of the recipes include exotic spices or seasonings. If you cannot obtain the required seasoning, be creative and substitute another.

So whether you are looking for new additions to your cooking repertoire or for time-saving, inexpensive meals, you are sure to find an array of irresistible recipes on the following pages.

Joie Warner

Basics

WING TIPS

HOW TO BUY CHICKEN WINGS
The first and most important step in making good wings is to purchase the freshest and plumpest wings you can find. Fresh wings have smooth skin with no discoloration and have a very faint and fresh-smelling aroma. Any slight off odor and you know they are past their prime. Ignore these and find a butcher with a good turnover, especially one that sells a lot of wings. I buy my wings in a Chinatown shop that does a brisk business in chicken wings and they are half the regular price. They are always piled high, packed on ice, and accessible, so it is easy for me to hand-pick (and sniff) the wings as I go along. This allows me to pick plumper and similar-sized wings for myself. If you do not live near a large Chinese community, you will have to find a good butcher and explain to him that you want only the freshest and meatiest wings available.

If you prefer to buy from your local supermarket, make sure that any wings you buy have not been previously frozen and that there is not a lot of blood accumulated in the bottom of the container (if there is, they have been

around awhile). Lastly, break open the plastic covering and take a good sniff — it is the only way to know if they are absolutely fresh. It is better than getting home and finding they are a bit off.

QUANTITIES AND BEST SIZE (AMOUNT TO THE POUND)
I have found that the best amount of wings to purchase for 2 to 4 people is approximately 14 wings, which when trimmed and separated gives you a total of 28 pieces. The weight will be approximately 2½ pounds for medium-sized wings. This is usually plenty when accompanied by a salad or side order. Buy another ½ pound for really hearty appetites.

Therefore; 2½ pounds = 14 wings = 28 pieces = 2 to 4 servings; 3¾ pounds = 21 wings = 42 pieces = 4 to 6 servings; and so on. Obviously, not all wings are the same weight or size, but generally this is how many wings I buy per serving.

TO STORE WINGS
Once purchased, wings should be immediately refrigerated or frozen. They should not be refrigerated any longer than a day and if you are freezing them, place them in freezer bags and seal tightly. They may be stored in the freezer section of your refrigerator for

around 1 month or for 2 to 3 months in a deep freezer.

I buy 10 or more pounds of wings at a time, count out 14, place in a freezer bag, and continue until all are bagged in portions for 2 to 4 and freeze. To thaw, I just remove 1 or 2 bags from the freezer and thaw for several hours at room temperature. While they are still slightly frozen in the center I remove the wings from the bag, pulling apart the still slightly frozen ones, and begin to trim them for cooking. Then, if I am not quite ready to use them, I refrigerate them or put them in a bowl with their marinade. Never refreeze wings once thawed.

HOW TO TRIM WINGS   Most of the following recipes instruct you to have wings trimmed and separated into two sections. You will find that they are easier to trim when still slightly frozen. Toss the sections into a large bowl with the premixed marinade, if you are using one.

I trim away the excess skin and fat to rid them of unnecessary fat and calories. I do not normally cut off the wing tips (why cut off the best part?), as one is generally told to do in other cookbooks, unless of course for Famous Buffalo Style Wings or if I am cooking for a crowd. Removing the wing tips allows room for more wings on the broiler or barbecue or in the deep-fryer.

The tips are often removed because they brown or become slightly charred before the rest of the wing is cooked. The tips are usually discarded or saved for soup stock. But millions of Chinese and some non-Chinese like myself enjoy this part of the wing. It is chewy and crunchy, albeit slightly overcooked — but then this is what makes it such a tasty tidbit, particularly to those who enjoy gnawing and chewing on well-cooked chicken bones. To cut off and discard the wing tip or not is your decision, but true wing aficionados would not think of it!

Here is how to trim: Examine the wings for feathers and pluck any off. Using a very sharp knife and holding wing up with its "elbow" resting on a chopping block, cut away the triangle or weblike skin as shown in diagram, and discard. Be careful not to remove any of the meat while doing this.

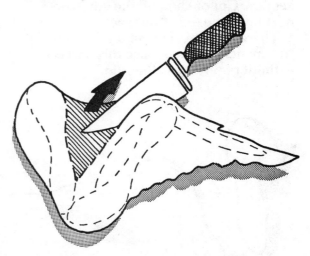

Next, grasp both wing sections and force them apart at the joint by bending them backward, which will loosen the bones. Cut between the two sections and you will now have two separate pieces: one that looks like a miniature drumstick, the other still looking like a wing.

13

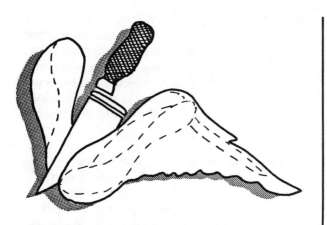

Now trim away the excess "frilly" skin around the outer edge of the "winglike" section. Cut or chop off the fatty end portion at the top of this section.

There is a fatty deposit on the skin of the "drumstick" section. Slice this part off without removing all the skin.

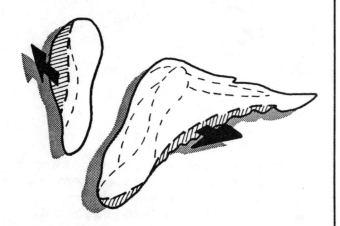

HOW TO TRIM BUFFALO STYLE
Trim according to the instructions above

but cut off total wing tip and discard or reserve tips for soup stock.

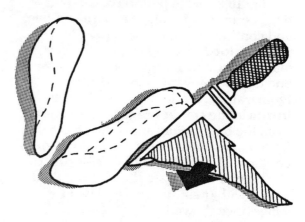

HOW TO BONE AND STUFF Trim and separate wings according to the instructions above and set aside the "drumsticks" to use in another recipe.

Using a sharp knife, slice around the top of the wing to loosen the skin and cut through the ligaments between the two

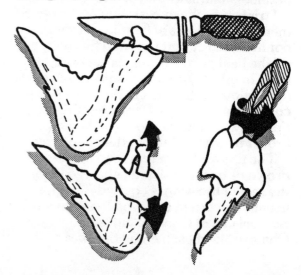

wing bones.

Scrape and push the meat down the length of the bones, then twist the bones off and discard.

Stuff wings with the recipe on page 40 or with your own stuffing.

MARINATING Marinating wings affects both the flavor and the texture of the meat. The liquid and seasonings penetrate the flesh, giving the skin and the flesh their distinctive taste while preventing the meat from drying out. The marinade almost always contains an acid such as fruit juice, wine, or vinegar, which is the tenderizer, along with spices to enhance the flavor and oil to keep the meat moist.

Because wings are small, they need not be marinated much longer than a couple of hours; if they are left too long some seasonings will be too intense. You may, of course, marinate wings in the refrigerator for several hours, or overnight if necessary, although the flavor will be stronger. Some people might prefer this, but some wings are supposed to be subtly flavored.

If you are cooking fewer wings than a recipe requires, do not reduce the amount of marinade ingredients or you will throw off the balance. If you wish to add a few more wings to the recipe, it is not necessary to add more marinade. Any more than a few, though, and you will have to double or triple the marinade accordingly.

It is best to premix the marinade ingredients in a large noncorrosive bowl, such as glass, ceramic, or stainless steel, then add wings and turn well in marinade to coat evenly. Do not cover the bowl, but if you must leave them to marinate longer than 2 hours, cover them and refrigerate until needed. Stir wings several times while they are marinating to insure that they are evenly flavored.

COOKING TIMES Cooking times are based on medium-sized wings, so you should adjust your cooking time based on whether your wings are small or large. Subtract around 5 minutes from my cooking times if your wings are quite tiny; add 5 minutes if very large.

When broiling or barbecuing, you may pierce a wing with a small knife to check if the meat is cooked through and there is no blood. I personally do not use this method, but instead usually judge doneness by just looking at the wings. If they look cooked, they usually are. They look cooked when both sides are golden brown and the wing tips are dark brown (by this I do not mean heavily charred black) with a few dark brown patches scattered across the skin. Do watch carefully because wings are easily overcooked. However, sometimes I have accidentally let them broil a bit too long and thought I had ruined them, only to find them still quite edible as long as they were not absolutely blackened and dried out.

When deep-frying or using another cooking method, you may also use the knife-piercing trick to check doneness or you may trust your eyes. Eventually one can just tell these things — especially if you have cooked as many chicken wings as I

15

have! (Just for testing recipes for this book, I have cooked somewhere between 300 to 400 pounds, which is about 2,000 wings. I promise it will not take that many wings to become an expert.)

BROILING AND BARBECUING All broiling and barbecuing recipes are interchangeable.

Broiling or barbecuing is the most succulent and flavorful way to cook wings. The distinctive flavor and crispy skin are brought about by high heat intensity and the marinating process, which infuses the meat with whatever seasonings you have selected.

To broil: preheat the broiler at least 15 minutes before using. Place the wings on a broiling rack that has a bottom pan in which to catch the drippings. Brush or spoon some of the marinade over wings, then place the rack so that the wings are about 6 inches away from the broiling element. The wings need to be turned only once, approximately 10 minutes after they have been under the broiler or on the grill. Brush or spoon marinade over them once more and cook another 5 or 10 minutes or until done.

To charcoal-grill: start your barbecue around a ½ hour to 40 minutes before you plan to cook the wings. Once the charcoal is coated with white ash, spread the coals out evenly. Place the grill over coals and allow it to heat before adding wings. Brush grill with oil first to prevent sticking. Add wings and cook as specified for broiling.

BAKING, PAN-FRYING, AND STIR-

FRYING Baking, pan-frying, and stir-frying take a little longer to cook, about 25 to 45 minutes, than broiling, barbecuing, and deep-frying because the heat is more intense in the latter methods of cooking.

WINGDING: WINGS FOR A CROWD, PARTY, OR PICNIC Wings are ideal party and picnic food — crowd pleasers while still easy on the cook. Any and all recipes in this book are great casual party fare.

If you are cooking for a large crowd, it is easier to barbecue because you can have everything ready (several bowls of different types of wings sitting in their marinades) and then barbecue as many as will fit at one time on the grill, continuing over the next few hours until all are done. Most people are happy to relieve the cook and take over the barbecue, which makes it quite a nice way to entertain.

Otherwise you can cook up as many wings as you like the day before the party and then serve them at room temperature the following day.

My favorite way of serving wings, whether at a party or for myself and husband, is having at least three or four different kinds, 2 broiled, 1 deep-fried, and another either pan-fried or stir-fried or braised. It is great fun to feast on the different flavored wings. Try this yourself because it is less complicated than it sounds.

Let us say you want to serve 2 to 4 people and choose to cook Parmesan Dijon Wings along with Soy Orange Wings. Prepare the two recipes, reducing the amount of wings in each by half (or 1¼ pounds wings per recipe). This gives you 2½ pounds of wings but with two different tastes. Do not cut marinade ingredients in half.

Start the Parmesan Dijon Wings in a frying pan on top of the stove at the same time you start broiling the Soy Orange Wings in the broiler or on the barbecue. If the wings are of similar size, most recipes will end up taking about the same time, whatever way they are cooked. If one dish is done a bit before the other, turn off the heat and allow it to stand while completing the other wings.

If you want to cook 2 different broiled wings, reduce the amount as described above without reducing the marinades, and place one type of wings on one side of the broiling pan and the other next to them. You can do this and still cook a third type on top of the stove, if you wish.

For a large crowd, serve more than one salad or side order. Do it sort of Chinese-style: for every 1 or 2 people, make up one more dish. Serve Old-Fashioned Potato Salad and Tarragon Macaroni Salad and add some Maple Ginger Beans. All of these dishes can be made ahead and, in the case of Maple Ginger Beans, it just needs reheating. If you still need more, boil up some corn on the cob and make some Herb Butter to slather on.

By the way, this makes a wonderfully festive indoor picnic, even in the middle of winter.

Note: Most of the wings may be served at room temperature (never cold) unless they are deep-fried or cooked in a lot of sauce. I have made a note at the end of any recipe where the flavor is enhanced if served at room temperature.

WING ETIQUETTE Wings are user-friendly. No need for knives, forks, or chopsticks. A pair of hands and a hearty appetite are all that are needed to experience the gustatory delights of chicken wings. Provide everyone with finger bowls — any small bowl filled with hot water and a slice of lemon to cut the grease — and lots of napkins and urge everyone to dig in and enjoy.

It is quite proper to pick up wings with the fingers (how else could you eat them?). Proceed to nibble, gnaw, and chew away until all the meat and flavorings have been completely savored. It is perfectly correct to ignore the table napkins and finger bowls and lick your fingers to remove the sauce. The more moans of delight and licking and smacking noises heard, the more compliments to the chef. This is where, after all, the terms lip-smackin' and finger-lickin' good came from.

INGREDIENTS

All recipes in the book have been tested using the following ingredients. Please use fresh, quality ingredients because they provide the best taste.

BLACK BEANS: These pungent, fermented, and salted black beans add a delicious flavor to many Chinese dishes. They are available in Chinese food shops.

BLACK PEPPER: Every recipe here uses black pepper, never white. It should always be freshly ground. Pepper already ground and sold in spice bottles is old and flavorless. Do not reduce the amount called for in any of the recipes even though it may seem like a lot of pepper. If anything, you might want to add more.

BUTTER: Cold fresh salted or unsalted butter should always be used. (Do not use margarine.) Butter that has been unrefrigerated for any length of time is invariably rancid. Not only is it not suitable for cooking or eating, but it is extremely bad for your health. Keep butter in the refrigerator to keep it fresh and remove it only when needed.

CHICKEN BROTH: A good, strong-flavored, homemade broth is excellent but, not having this, you may substitute a good-quality canned chicken broth.

CRUSHED RED PEPPER FLAKES: These dried, crushed red peppers must be absolutely fresh or they will have lost both their bite and their flavor.

CURRY POWDER: Asian cooks usually prepare their own curry powder from numerous spices and so do I, but the commercial blends may be used in any of these recipes. Just be sure to buy a quality brand.

DRIED HERBS AND SPICES: Chuck out all your old, stale spices and use only freshly bought ones. Bottled spices and herbs get stale very quickly and if used are guaranteed to make your dishes turn out dull and bland.

DURKEE RED HOT CAYENNE PEPPER SAUCE: Hereinafter referred to as Durkee Red Hot sauce. The secret ingredient in Famous Buffalo Style Wings and in many other dishes as well, this beautifully full-flavored hot sauce made from fully aged cayenne pepper mash, vinegar, salt, and garlic is becoming more and more readily available in supermarkets. If a recipe calls for it and you do not have it, you may substitute other hot sauces such as Tabasco or sambal oelek — except in Famous Buffalo Style Wings — but there will be a slight change in flavor. Every recipe gives the order of preference for all the hot sauces.

FIVE SPICE POWDER: Use this strong powder judiciously. It is a combination of spices, usually star anise, cinnamon, cloves, fennel, and Szechuan peppercorns. It is available in Oriental food shops.

GARLIC: Never use garlic powder and do not buy those terrible little garlic bulbs that are sold two to a package. Buy them individually and if your food store does not sell them that way, find one that does. Garlic is an important flavor in these recipes, and if the bulbs are stale, shriveled, and sprouting they will ruin the dish.

You will notice that most of my recipes call for large garlic cloves. Do not be afraid to use a lot of garlic — my philosophy is: When in doubt, add more!

A large clove of garlic is a healthy ½ tablespoon. If necessary, substitute 3 or 4 small cloves to make 1 large. Also, read the instructions carefully to know whether you chop or mince garlic because the flavor of the dish depends on this. Most recipes instruct you to chop, which means leaving them in fairly large pieces, but a few require you to mince them finely.

GINGER: Use fresh ginger unless otherwise specified. There is no need to peel the ginger for these recipes; just mince finely. When ground ginger is called for, use a good-quality brand. It should have a good, strong aroma of ginger. I use a brand called Abdullah's, which is available in some gourmet shops and supermarkets.

HOISIN SAUCE: This is a thick, brownish-red paste that tastes sweet, spicy, and slightly hot. It is available in Oriental food shops and some gourmet and grocery stores.

HONEY: Mild liquid honey is used in these recipes. Do not use flavored honeys or they will mask the other flavors.

LEMON JUICE: Use fresh-squeezed juice only, never bottled.

LIQUID SMOKE: This concentrated liquid form of smoke used to give food a smoky flavor is manufactured by burning damp wood, usually hickory. The smoke is then condensed and processed to remove all the harmful tars and resins. It is available in the spice department in supermarkets.

MAPLE SYRUP: Be sure it is 100 percent pure maple syrup. Anything less will not do.

MIRIN AND DRY SHERRY: Mirin (Aji-Mirin) is a sweet cooking rice wine used in Japanese cooking. I use it in both Chinese and Japanese recipes instead of rice wine or dry sherry. If you prefer, you may use dry sherry but only the pale type.

MUSTARD: I use both Dijon-type (Maille brand) and French's Bold 'n Spicy Deli Mustard in my recipes. They may be interchanged, but I have put them in order of preference in the recipes that require mustard.

OLIVE OIL: Use only mild, light olive oil because dark green olive oils are too strongly flavored and will mask the other ingredients.

OYSTER SAUCE: This pungent, delicious sauce is made from oyster extract and seasonings. It is available in Oriental food shops and some gourmet and grocery stores.

PARMESAN CHEESE: Never use the powdered sawdust that is sold in supermarkets in cylindrical cardboard containers. It is terrible and does not resemble the real thing at all. Instead, buy real Parmesan cheese. I buy a large wedge; although it may seem expensive, it lasts well and the authentic flavor is worth the price. The rind should read "Parmigiano Reggiano" or, second best, "Grana Padano." It is available in Italian grocery stores or well-stocked cheese stores. Keep it refrigerated in a plastic bag and grate it just before using. Some gourmet shops sell it already ground. Do not buy it, it is dried out and flavorless.

PLUM SAUCE: This thick, sweet sauce made from plums, ginger, chili, and seasonings is available in Oriental food shops and some gourmet and grocery stores. Use only brands manufactured in the Orient; the domestic brands are much too sweet.

SAMBAL OELEK: This is a bottled preparation of crushed red peppers and salt used in Indonesian cooking. I use it in all my cooking when recipes call for fresh hot red peppers and I do not have any. It is easy to use: 1 to 2 teaspoons for every 2 ground chilies called for in a recipe. A brand I use is Go-Tan, made in Holland. It is available in Oriental food shops and some gourmet shops.

SESAME OIL: Use only Chinese or Japanese sesame oil. A good brand is Kadoya, made in Japan. It is available in Oriental food shops and some gourmet and grocery stores. Avoid the kinds in plastic bottles; they are usually quite rancid-tasting. Nor should the type available in health food stores be substituted because it is quite different.

SOY SAUCE: All recipes in this book were tested using Kikkoman soy sauce. You may use other Oriental soy sauces, but never use the domestic brands sold in supermarkets because they are chemically, not naturally, fermented.

STAR ANISE: This star-shaped seed cluster with a licorice taste is found in Oriental food shops. Do not substitute the Western spice anise.

SZECHUAN PEPPERCORNS: This aromatic, reddish-brown spice is used frequently in Szechuanese cooking and can be purchased in Oriental food shops.

TABASCO SAUCE: This liquid form of cayenne peppers is called for in a few recipes and can be used as a substitute (except in Famous Buffalo Style Wings) in most recipes calling for Durkee Red Hot sauce.

VINEGAR: White vinegar is used in my recipes unless otherwise stated. Some call for red wine vinegar or rice vinegar, which is a mild Japanese vinegar found in Oriental food shops.

EQUIPMENT

BROILING RACK: A broiling rack consists of two pieces; a top rack with slots and a bottom pan to catch the drippings. Many recipes in this book rely on this piece of equipment, and because broiling allows the wings to sit away from the fat drippings, it makes it a healthier way of cooking.

FRYING PAN: A large heavy frying pan is essential for a few recipes. Cast iron is the best and it should be at least 12 inches in diameter for both pan-frying and deep-frying. Enameled frying pans are not as good because foods do not brown well in them. Do not use flimsy aluminum or stainless steel pans because food is guaranteed to stick and burn in them at high frying temperatures.

KNIVES: Knives should be sharp, sharp, sharp.

SAUCEPAN: Again, a saucepan should be heavy, not flimsy, or you will have food burning and sticking to the bottom.

TONGS: These are very useful for turning over wings. Long-handled tongs are preferable for reaching into the oven or over a hot barbecue.

WOK: A heavy cast-iron wok is the best and it should be at least 14 inches in diameter. Second best is rolled steel. Stainless steel should not be used because it does not conduct heat as well. Always heat your wok on the stove for a few minutes before adding oil for stir-frying. This prevents food from sticking to it.

ALL-TIME FAVORITE WINGS

Famous Buffalo Style

WINGS

Craig Claiborne called Buffalo chicken wings the "best new regional dish in years." Food writer Bert Greene calls them an outstanding culinary contribution, and Calvin Trillin, unconventional food journalist and author, says he has tried Buffalo chicken wings mild, medium, and hot and he has found there is no sort of chicken wing he does not like. I agree. You do not have to go to Buffalo to enjoy them. They are incredibly easy to make yourself. Be sure to serve them with a side order of crispy celery sticks and Blue Cheese Dressing. It helps put out the fire!

CELERY STICKS
1 bunch celery

1. Separate stalks and wash celery.
2. Trim the leafy tops and the root end. Cut the celery in half and then into thin strips. Soak in ice water in refrigerator until needed.

BLUE CHEESE DRESSING
2 ounces blue cheese, crumbled
½ cup homemade or Hellman's mayonnaise
½ cup sour cream

1. Place everything in food processor and process until smooth. Chill.

Serves 4

BUFFALO STYLE WINGS
2½ pounds wings, trimmed and
separated Buffalo style
¼ cup (½ stick) butter
3 to 5 tablespoons Durkee Red Hot sauce
1 tablespoon vinegar (optional)
oil for deep-frying

1. Prepare celery sticks and blue cheese dressing and chill.
2. Slowly melt butter in a large noncorrosive saucepan. Add Durkee Red Hot sauce (3 tablespoons for mild, 4 tablespoons for medium, more for hot, and much much more for suicide! I suggest you start off with mild, which is still quite hot, and then try it hotter next time if you like). Add vinegar, if using, and remove from heat.
3. Heat oil in a large heavy frying pan to about 370°. Deep-fry wings, a few at a time until nicely browned and crisp, about 10 to 15 minutes. Remove to a paper-towel-lined plate to drain.
4. Immediately reheat butter sauce and add wings to saucepan. Toss to coat evenly and transfer to a platter.
5. Serve with icy cold celery sticks and Blue Cheese Dressing on the side.

Serves 2 to 4

Note: The above recipe is the classic way — the following is my way: Brush both sides of wings with vegetable oil and place on broiling rack. Broil 15 to 20 minutes or until nicely crisped. Meanwhile melt ¼ cup butter, 4½ tablespoons Durkee Red Hot sauce, and 2 tablespoons red wine vinegar in a large saucepan. Add wings to saucepan and immediately toss them in the sauce. Transfer to a platter and serve.

The secret ingredient!

Texas Style Barbecued

WINGS

*Incredible barbecued flavor whether barbecued
out of doors over coals, or indoors in a broiler.*

2½ pounds wings, trimmed and separated
½ cup vegetable oil
3 cups chopped onions
5 large garlic cloves, chopped
1 can (28 ounces) tomatoes, drained
1 can (5½ ounces) tomato paste
2 teaspoons sambal oelek or Tabasco sauce
2 tablespoons dry mustard
2 tablespoons sugar
1 tablespoon red wine vinegar
1½ teaspoons salt
1 teaspoon freshly ground black pepper

1. Heat oil in a large, heavy noncorrosive frying pan. Fry onions and garlic in oil until soft but not brown, about 5 minutes.
2. Add remaining ingredients and bring to a boil. Reduce heat slightly and boil sauce, stirring constantly until thickened enough to coat a spoon, about 10 minutes.
3. Start barbecue or preheat broiler.
4. Add wings to sauce and bring to a boil. Stir constantly in sauce and reduce heat to low. Continue to cook wings in sauce, about 10 minutes.
5. Place wings, coated with some of the sauce, on grill or broiling rack and cook until wings are browned and slightly charred, about 10 to 15 minutes, turning once and basting with sauce.
6. Transfer to a platter and serve.

Serves 2 to 4

Crispy Breaded
WINGS

Crispy and crunchy on the outside, moist and juicy on the inside — yummy! Dip wings in Horseradish–Sour Cream Dip or Mild, Medium, or Molten Dip.

2½ pounds wings, trimmed and separated
2 cups flour
2 cups fine dry bread crumbs
2 eggs, well beaten with 2 tablespoons water
salt and pepper
vegetable oil for deep-frying

1. Place flour on a piece of waxed paper and bread crumbs on another piece.
2. Set bowl of eggwash next to flour and bread crumbs. Salt and pepper wings.
3. Coat wings first in flour, dip in eggwash, then in bread crumbs, making certain they are evenly covered.
4. Heat oil in a heavy deep frying pan to about 370°. Fry as many wings as will fit in pan without crowding. Cook until nicely browned and cooked through, about 10 to 15 minutes.
5. Transfer to a paper-towel-lined plate to drain and continue with remaining wings until all are done.
6. Transfer to a platter and serve with dips.

Serves 2 to 4

Honey Garlic
WINGS

The honey-garlic flavor combination is particularly pleasing to just about everyone who tastes it. Invented by the Cantonese, this recipe is probably one of the oldest chicken wing recipes around. I guess that would make it a classic.

2½ pounds wings, trimmed and separated
⅓ cup soy sauce
3 tablespoons mild honey
¾ cup water
vegetable oil for stir-frying
4 large garlic cloves, chopped
2 teaspoons minced fresh ginger

1. Combine the soy sauce, honey, and water in a small bowl.
2. Heat wok and add a little oil. When hot, add garlic and ginger and stir-fry a second or two. Add wings and stir-fry until nicely browned, about 5 minutes, adding more oil if necessary.
3. Add soy sauce mixture and turn heat down to simmer. Cover and cook 20 to 25 minutes or until wings are cooked through. Lift lid and stir occasionally.
4. Remove lid and turn heat up to high. Cook wings, stirring all the while, until sauce is reduced enough to glaze wings.
5. Transfer to a platter and serve.

Serves 2 to 4

BARBECUED WINGS

Lemon Garlic Pepper

WINGS

Peppery and piquant, these wings are absolutely
scrumptious. Although it may seem like a lot of
pepper, do not reduce the amount called for.
You will also notice that the marinade ingredients
are not mixed together first but instead poured
over the wings separately.
Add ingredients in order given, before mixing, or
the lemony flavor will be lost.

2½ pounds wings, trimmed and separated
½ cup lemon juice
5 to 6 large garlic cloves, chopped
1 tablespoon crushed black peppercorns
2 teaspoons salt
¼ cup olive oil

1. Place wings in large glass or enamel bowl and pour over lemon juice, garlic, and crushed peppercorns.
2. Sprinkle on salt and pour olive oil over wings and stir.
3. Marinate for 2 hours at room temperature, stirring occasionally to coat wings with marinade. Drain and reserve marinade.
4. Start barbecue or preheat broiler. Place wings on grill and barbecue until browned, about 15 to 20 minutes. Turn after 10 minutes and baste with marinade.
5. Transfer to a platter and serve.

Serves 2 to 4

Drunken
WINGS

Do not be alarmed at the appearance of these superlative wings. Although they are heavily charred, they are still very moist and tender.

2½ pounds wings, trimmed and separated
4 large garlic cloves, chopped
1 medium onion, minced
½ cup light rum
2 tablespoons soy sauce
2 teaspoons Worcestershire sauce
4 tablespoons olive oil
3 tablespoons mild honey
2 teaspoons Durkee Red Hot sauce or to taste

1. Mix marinade ingredients in a bowl large enough to accommodate wings. Add wings, stir, and marinate for 2 hours at room temperature. Drain and reserve marinade.
2. Start barbecue or preheat broiler. Place wings on grill and barbecue until browned and cooked through, about 15 to 20 minutes. Turn after 10 minutes and baste with marinade.
3. Transfer to a platter and serve.

Serves 2 to 4

Bad Bernie's Barbecued
WINGS

*These wings are lip-smackin', finger-lickin' good.
They are not really barbecued but instead are
tossed in a barbecue sauce.*

2½ pounds wings, trimmed and separated
⅔ cup ketchup
½ cup white vinegar
½ cup water
1 tablespoon sugar
2 tablespoons Bold 'n Spicy or
Dijon-type mustard
2 tablespoons butter
1 teaspoon salt
2 tablespoons Worcestershire sauce
2 teaspoons sambal oelek, Durkee Red Hot
sauce, or Tabasco sauce
vegetable oil for deep-frying

1. Mix sauce ingredients in a large, heavy noncorrosive saucepan and bring to the boil. Reduce heat slightly and simmer, stirring occasionally for 20 minutes.
2. Heat oil in a large heavy frying pan to about 370°. Deep-fry wings, a few at a time, until nicely browned and cooked through, approximately 10 to 15 minutes.
3. Transfer to paper-towel-lined plate to drain, then place wings in pan with barbecue sauce.
4. Stir wings in sauce for a few seconds to heat.
5. Transfer to a platter and serve.

Serves 2 to 4

**Bad Bernie's Barbecued Wings, a mug of beer, and
a side order of deep-fried onion rings**

Drew's Dynamite
WINGS

My husband Drew walked into the kitchen one day and concocted this fabulous marinade on the spur of the moment. It only works with fresh rosemary and fresh basil. Do not bother to make it with dried herbs — it will not be the same.

2½ pounds wings, trimmed and separated
3 large garlic cloves, chopped
½ cup olive oil
3½ tablespoons red wine vinegar
4 tablespoons Durkee Red Hot sauce
4 teaspoons Worcestershire sauce
3 tablespoons (1½ ounces) Canadian whisky
½ teaspoon salt
1 teaspoon freshly ground black pepper
3 tablespoons chopped fresh rosemary leaves
1 tablespoon chopped fresh basil leaves

1. Mix marinade ingredients in a large bowl. Add wings, stir, and marinate for 2 hours at room temperature. Drain and reserve marinade.
2. Start barbecue or preheat broiler. Place wings on grill and barbecue until browned and cooked through, about 15 to 20 minutes. Turn after 10 minutes and baste with marinade.
3. Transfer to a platter and serve.

Serves 2 to 4

ORIENTAL WINGS

Hot Sesame
WINGS

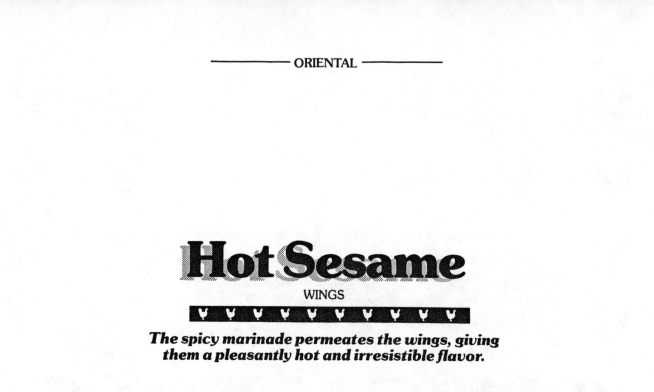

The spicy marinade permeates the wings, giving them a pleasantly hot and irresistible flavor.

2½ pounds wings, trimmed and separated
1 tablespoon minced fresh ginger
2 large garlic cloves, chopped
¼ cup soy sauce
4 tablespoons mild honey
3 tablespoons mirin or dry sherry
1 tablespoon rice vinegar
5 teaspoons sambal oelek or Tabasco sauce
1 tablespoon sesame oil
2 tablespoons sesame seeds

1. Mix marinade ingredients in a bowl large enough to accommodate wings. Add wings, stir, and marinate for 2 hours at room temperature. Drain and reserve marinade.
2. Preheat broiler. Place wings on broiling rack and broil 15 to 20 minutes or until browned. Turn after 10 minutes and baste with marinade.
3. Transfer to a platter and serve.

Serves 2 to 4

Braised Orange
WINGS

*Alive with the flavor of orange, these should be
served with rice to soak up the marvelous sauce.*

2½ pounds wings, trimmed and separated
2½ tablespoons soy sauce
2½ tablespoons mirin or dry sherry
2 tablespoons hoisin sauce
1½ cups chicken broth
4 teaspoons cornstarch
4 teaspoons water
vegetable oil for stir-frying
2 small onions, chopped
3 large garlic cloves, chopped
2 tablespoons minced fresh ginger
rind of 2 large oranges, white
membrane removed, and finely chopped
2 teaspoons sambal oelek
1 teaspoon sesame oil

1. Mix soy sauce, mirin, hoisin sauce, and chicken broth in a bowl.
2. Mix cornstarch and water in another small bowl.
3. Heat wok and add oil. When hot, add half the wings and stir-fry until browned on both sides. Remove to a casserole dish just large enough to accommodate wings. Add remaining wings and fry until browned. Remove to casserole.
4. Add onions, garlic, ginger, orange rind, and sambal oelek to wok and stir-fry until onions are translucent. Add more oil if needed.
5. Transfer onion mixture to casserole and pour seasoning liquid over it. Bring to a boil on top of stove, cover, and reduce heat to medium low.
6. Simmer for 20 minutes, remove lid, and stir wings. Cover again and cook another 15 to 20 minutes.
7. Stir cornstarch mixture, remove lid, and add to casserole. Stir on heat until thickened. Add sesame oil, stir, and serve.

Serves 2 to 4

Tea Smoked
WINGS

This recipe requires a large heavy cast-iron or carbon steel wok, not a stainless steel or aluminum wok, because they are too flimsy for the smoking process. A complicated recipe, yes, but the wings have a wonderful delicate and sophisticated quality.

2½ pounds wings, trimmed and separated Buffalo Style
1 teaspoon salt
2 teaspoons Szechuan peppercorns, finely crushed
½ teaspoon five spice powder
1 tablespoon mirin or dry sherry
¼ cup loose black tea leaves
¼ cup brown sugar
rind of 1 medium orange, white membrane removed, and torn into small pieces
3 star anise, broken into pieces
2 teaspoons sesame oil

1. Mix salt, Szechuan peppercorns, five spice powder, and mirin in a bowl. Rub this mixture over wings and marinate for 2 hours at room temperature.
2. Fill a large wok with hot tap water to the level of a rack placed in the wok to hold a plate. Bring water to a rolling boil.
3. Place wings on a heat-proof plate and, wearing oven mitts to protect hands from steam, place plate on center of rack.
4. Cover the wok tightly and steam wings 10 to 15 minutes over high heat. Wearing oven mitts, remove plate of wings from wok. Discard marinade and set wings aside to cool.
5. Dry wok and line the inside with 4 layers

of aluminum foil. The foil layers should be touching the bottom of wok. Line the wok lid with another 4 layers of aluminum foil.

6. Combine tea leaves, brown sugar, orange rind, and star anise in bowl. Pour mixture on bottom of foil-covered wok. Lightly oil the rack and place over smoking mixture. Place the wings on rack, allowing room between each wing for smoke to circulate.

7. Cover wok tightly with lid. Place wok directly on burner and turn heat to high. Wait until you detect the smell of smoke and time the wings for 5 minutes, then turn off heat. Leave wok covered for another 10 minutes.

8. Remove wings and brush with a little sesame oil.

9. Transfer to a platter and serve at room temperature. The wings may be done ahead of time, refrigerated, then brought to room temperature before serving.

Serves 2 to 4

*These are best served at room temperature.

Tea Smoked Wings

Plum Sauce
WINGS

Sauce and wings go into the pot all at once.
Nothing could be simpler — and very tasty too.

2½ pounds wings, trimmed and separated
½ cup Chinese plum sauce
⅓ cup water
3 teaspoons minced fresh ginger
3 tablespoons dry sherry
½ teaspoon soy sauce
1 teaspoon sambal oelek or Tabasco sauce

1. **Place everything except wings in a heavy saucepan large enough to accommodate wings. Stir to mix well.**
2. **Add wings and toss to coat evenly.**
3. **Bring to a boil, reduce heat to medium, cover, and cook, stirring frequently, for 20 to 25 minutes or until cooked.**
4. **Remove lid and cook another 5 minutes, stirring all the while, until wings are nicely glazed. You may have to turn the heat up a bit to accomplish this; there should not be any sauce left, only a nice caramelized coating on each wing.**
5. **Transfer to a platter and serve.**

Serves 2 to 4

Peanut Butter
WINGS

Peanut butter is used as a seasoning in a number of Asian countries, Indonesia in particular. I had to set aside my own prejudices and give these wings a try. They were a pleasant surprise.

2½ pounds wings, trimmed and separated
¼ cup peanut butter
2 teaspoons curry powder
½ teaspoon salt
½ teaspoon freshly ground black pepper
4 tablespoons fresh lemon juice
1 tablespoon brown sugar
3 tablespoons soy sauce
2 tablespoons minced fresh ginger
3 large garlic cloves, chopped
1 tablespoon peanut oil
½ teaspoon Tabasco sauce, sambal oelek, or Durkee Red Hot sauce

1. Mix marinade ingredients in a large bowl. Add wings, stir, and marinate for 2 hours at room temperature. Drain and reserve marinade.
2. Preheat broiler. Place wings on broiling rack and broil 15 to 20 minutes or until browned. Turn after 10 minutes and baste with marinade.
3. Transfer to a platter and serve.

Serves 2 to 4

Thai Stuffed

WINGS

These spectacular boned and stuffed wings have exotic flavors from Thailand. Boning and stuffing the wings is a simple yet time-consuming technique (see instructions on page 14) for which you will need a good sharp knife. Once it is mastered, you can devise a number of tasty stuffings yourself. The wings may be stuffed ahead of time, refrigerated, then dipped in cornstarch and deep-fried just before serving. The fish sauce (nam pla) is an optional ingredient and can be purchased in Oriental food shops carrying Vietnamese and Thai food items.

2½ pounds wings, trimmed, separated, and boned
½ pound ground pork
1 teaspoon sambal oelek or crushed red pepper flakes
1 large garlic clove, minced
2 tablespoons minced parsley
5 water chestnuts, finely chopped
1 whole medium green onion, finely chopped
¼ teaspoon salt
½ teaspoon freshly ground black pepper
1 tablespoon mirin or dry sherry
1 tablespoon fish sauce (nam pla) or soy sauce
¼ cup cornstarch
vegetable oil for deep-frying

1. **Combine pork, sambal oelek, garlic, parsley, water chestnuts, green onions, salt, pepper, water, and fish sauce in a bowl.**
2. **Using fingers, stuff this mixture loosely into each wing cavity. Do not overstuff or the stuffing will not be properly cooked through when deep-fried.**
3. **Coat wings by rolling in cornstarch.**
4. **Heat oil to about 370°. Deep-fry wings, a few at a time, until golden brown, approximately 15 to 20 minutes. Remove to a paper-towel-lined plate to drain.**
5. **Transfer to a platter and serve with Soy Lemon Dip (see page 100).**

Serves 2 to 4

Soy Orange
WINGS

*The ravishing aroma of these wings marinating
gives a hint of the extraordinary taste treat to
come. These tend to brown quickly, be careful not
to burn them.*

2½ pounds wings, trimmed and separated
¼ cup soy sauce
½ cup orange juice, fresh or frozen
2 tablespoons mild honey
1 small onion, minced
1 tablespoon grated orange rind
1 teaspoon dry mustard
1 teaspoon curry powder
1 teaspoon sambal oelek or Tabasco sauce

**1. Combine everything except wings in a
large bowl. Add wings, stir, and marinate
for 2 hours at room temperature. Drain
and reserve marinade.
2. Preheat broiler. Place wings on broiling
rack and broil until nicely browned and
cooked through, about 15 to 20 minutes.
Turn after 10 minutes and baste with
marinade.
3. Transfer to a platter and serve.**

Serves 2 to 4

Oyster Sauce

WINGS

Your palate will be delighted by these savory, full-flavored wings. Old-Fashioned Potato Salad is good with this dish or you may serve rice.

2½ pounds wings, trimmed and separated
2 tablespoons soy sauce
1 tablespoon mirin or dry sherry
3½ tablespoons oyster sauce
½ cup chicken broth
½ teaspoon sesame oil
1 teaspoon cornstarch
1 tablespoon water
vegetable oil for stir-frying
4 teaspoons minced fresh ginger
2 large garlic cloves, chopped
3 whole medium green onions, chopped

1. Mix soy sauce, mirin, oyster sauce, chicken broth, and sesame oil in a bowl.
2. Mix cornstarch and water in another small bowl.
3. Heat wok and add oil. When hot, add half the wings and fry until browned on both sides, about 5 minutes. Remove to a plate. Add remaining wings and fry until browned.
4. Add ginger, garlic, and green onions and add the browned wings.
5. Stir seasoning liquid and add to wings. Bring to a boil and cover. Reduce heat to medium-low and simmer for 20 to 25 minutes, lifting lid and stirring occasionally.
6. Uncover, stir cornstarch mixture, and add to wok. Turn heat to high and stir until wings are glazed and sauce thickened.
7. Transfer to a platter and serve.

Serves 2 to 4

Indonesian
WINGS

These terrific-tasting, mildly hot wings require Indonesian sweet soy sauce, Ketjap Manis. It is not readily available in supermarkets but can be found in some Oriental food shops.

2½ pounds wings, trimmed and separated
4 large garlic cloves, chopped
3 teaspoons sambal oelek
4 teaspoons fresh lemon juice
2 tablespoons water
⅛ teaspoon five spice powder
4 tablespoons Ketjap Manis
2 teaspoons minced fresh ginger

1. Mix marinade ingredients in a bowl large enough to hold wings. Add wings, stir, and marinate for 2 hours at room temperature. Drain and reserve marinade.
2. Preheat broiler. Place wings on broiling rack and broil 15 to 20 minutes or until browned. Turn after 10 minutes and baste with marinade.
3. Transfer to a platter and serve.

Serves 2 to 4

Honey Ginger
WINGS

Prepare these with a mild honey; a strong honey will overpower the other seasonings.

2½ pounds wings, trimmed and separated
4 tablespoons fresh lemon juice
¼ cup soy sauce
3 tablespoons mild honey
3 tablespoons minced fresh ginger
½ teaspoon salt
¼ cup water

1. Mix marinade ingredients in a large bowl. Add wings, stir, and marinate for 2 hours at room temperature. Drain and reserve marinade.
2. Preheat broiler. Place wings on broiling rack and broil 15 to 20 minutes. Turn after 10 minutes and baste with marinade.
3. Transfer to a platter and serve.

Serves 2 to 4

Soy Sauce

WINGS

Pungent and earthy, these may be served hot or at room temperature. If done ahead and refrigerated, take them out of the refrigerator an hour before serving them.

2½ pounds wings, trimmed and separated
1 cup soy sauce
2 cups water
8 tablespoons sugar
¼ cup dry sherry
1 star anise, broken into pieces
3 large garlic cloves, chopped
2 tablespoons minced fresh ginger
2 whole medium green onions, quartered
¼ teaspoon sesame oil

1. Mix sauce ingredients in a saucepan large enough to accommodate wings. Bring liquid to a boil and add wings. Lower heat to simmer and cover.
2. Cook wings 15 to 20 minutes, lifting lid occasionally to stir wings. Turn off heat and allow wings to sit in the covered saucepan for 45 minutes. Lift lid occasionally and give wings a stir to color evenly. Add sesame oil.
3. To serve, reheat wings in sauce and transfer to a platter or serve at room temperature.

Serves 2 to 4

*These are best served at room temperature.

45

Black Bean Sauce

WINGS

These succulent wings have a beautiful hearty flavor of garlic and black beans. There is a lot of sauce, so serve rice alongside to soak up some of the delicious gravy.

2½ pounds wings, trimmed and separated
3 tablespoons black beans, rinsed and coarsely chopped
2 large garlic cloves, coarsely chopped
2 teaspoons minced fresh ginger
2 tablespoons soy sauce
2 tablespoons mirin or dry sherry
1 tablespoon oyster sauce
1 cup water
1½ tablespoons cornstarch
3 tablespoons water
vegetable oil for stir-frying
1 medium onion, coarsely chopped
1 medium green pepper, coarsely chopped
1 tablespoon sesame oil

1. Place black beans, garlic, and ginger in a small bowl.
2. In another bowl, mix soy sauce, mirin, oyster sauce, and 1 cup water.
3. Mix cornstarch and 3 tablespoons water in another bowl.
4. Heat wok and add a few tablespoons oil. When hot, add black beans, ginger, and garlic and stir-fry a few seconds.
5. Add onions and green pepper and stir-fry a few seconds more.
6. Add a bit more oil if needed and add wings. Stir-fry until browned nicely, about 5 to 10 minutes.
7. Add liquid seasoning, turn heat to simmer, cover, and cook for 15 to 20 minutes more, stirring occasionally.
8. Turn heat up to high, uncover, stir cornstarch mixture, and add to wok. Stir until wings are glazed and sauce is thickened.
9. Add sesame oil, stir to mix, and transfer to a platter and serve.

Serves 2 to 4

Black Bean Sauce Wings with rice

Chinese Barbecued

WINGS

Buy a good brand of hoisin sauce. It will guarantee the wings a nice tangy taste.

2½ pounds wings, trimmed and separated
½ cup soy sauce
1 large garlic clove, chopped
¼ cup hoisin sauce
¼ cup mirin or dry sherry
2 teaspoons minced fresh ginger
½ teaspoon five spice powder

1. Mix marinade ingredients in a bowl large enough to accommodate wings. Add wings, stir, and marinate for 2 hours at room temperature. Drain and reserve marinade.
2. Preheat broiler. Place wings on broiling rack and broil 15 to 20 minutes or until browned and cooked through. Turn after 10 minutes and baste with marinade.
3. Transfer to a platter and serve.

Serves 2 to 4

Hawaiian
WINGS

Spicy-sweet would describe these wings.
Familiar Oriental seasonings are used in many, if
not most, Hawaiian recipes.

2½ pounds wings, trimmed and separated
¼ cup soy sauce
⅛ cup plum sauce
1 tablespoon hoisin sauce
1 tablespoon white vinegar
2 tablespoons mild honey
2 large garlic cloves, chopped
2 teaspoons minced fresh ginger

1. Mix marinade ingredients well in a large bowl. Add wings, stir, and marinate for 2 hours at room temperature. Drain and reserve marinade.
2. Preheat broiler. Place wings on broiling rack and broil 15 to 20 minutes or until browned and cooked through. Turn after 10 minutes and baste with marinade.
3. Transfer to a platter and serve.

Serves 2 to 4

Honey Ketchup

WINGS

Keep an eye on these sweet and glossy wings while they are baking because they tend to burn easily.

2½ pounds wings, trimmed and separated
pinch of salt
pinch of freshly ground black pepper
1½ tablespoons peanut oil
2 tablespoons ketchup
⅓ cup mild honey
½ cup soy sauce
1 tablespoon mirin or dry white vermouth
1 large garlic clove, chopped

1. Preheat oven to 400°.
2. Mix sauce ingredients in a large bowl and add wings. Stir to coat well.
3. Pour wings and sauce into a baking dish and bake 30 to 35 minutes or until nicely caramelized. Reduce heat if wings begin to brown too quickly. Turn them once or twice while baking.
4. Transfer to a platter and serve.

Serves 2 to 4

WINGS

This marinade gives a distinctly Japanese taste to the wings. Bottled teriyaki sauce is available at some supermarkets and at most Oriental food shops.

2½ pounds wings, trimmed and separated
¾ cup bottled teriyaki sauce
½ cup pineapple juice
3 large garlic cloves, minced
⅛ teaspoon freshly ground black pepper

1. Mix marinade ingredients well in a large bowl. Add wings, stir, and marinate for 2 hours at room temperature. Drain and reserve marinade.
2. Preheat broiler. Place wings on broiling rack and broil 15 to 20 minutes or until browned and cooked through. Turn after 10 minutes and baste with marinade.
3. Transfer to a platter and serve.

Serves 2 to 4

Sweet and Sour

WINGS

Sweet and sour sauces served in Chinese restaurants are often cloying. However, when well made, the flavor is very appetizing. As with other saucy Oriental dishes, rice is a perfect accompaniment.

2½ pounds wings, trimmed and separated
1 cup water
3 tablespoons ketchup
3 tablespoons white vinegar
3 tablespoons sugar
2 teaspoons soy sauce
¼ teaspoon sesame oil
2 teaspoons cornstarch
vegetable oil for stir-frying
1 tablespoon minced fresh ginger
2 large garlic cloves, chopped

1. Mix water, ketchup, vinegar, sugar, soy sauce, sesame oil, and cornstarch in a bowl.
2. Heat wok and add oil. Add half the wings and fry until browned, about 5 minutes. Remove to a plate. Add remaining wings and fry until browned.
3. Add ginger and garlic and all the browned wings. Turn heat to medium and cook, stirring occasionally until done, about 25 to 30 minutes.
4. Stir seasoning liquid and add to wings. Bring to a boil on high heat and cook, stirring, until thickly glazed.
5. Transfer to a platter and serve.

Serves 2 to 4

Korean
WINGS

Do not try to reduce the amount of sugar in this recipe. The amount is necessary for the correct flavor.

2½ pounds wings, trimmed and separated
3 tablespoons soy sauce
3 tablespoons mirin or dry sherry
1½ tablespoons sugar
2 large garlic cloves, minced
2 teaspoons minced fresh ginger
2 teaspoons sesame seeds
1 tablespoon sesame oil
pinch of freshly ground black pepper

1. Mix marinade ingredients in a bowl large enough to hold wings. Add wings, stir, and marinate for 2 hours at room temperature. Drain and reserve marinade.
2. Preheat broiler. Place wings on broiling rack and broil until browned and cooked through, about 15 to 20 minutes. Turn after 10 minutes and baste with marinade.
3. Transfer to a platter and serve.

Serves 2 to 4

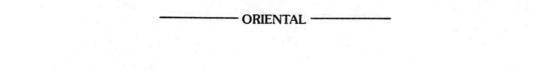

Lemony
WINGS

*A classic Cantonese dish that is lemony-tart and
perfect served with steamed rice.*

2½ pounds wings, trimmed and separated
4 tablespoons soy sauce
4 tablespoons mirin or dry sherry
½ cup chicken broth
grated rind of 1 large lemon
juice of 1 large lemon
3 tablespoons sugar
½ teaspoon salt
2 teaspoons water
2 teaspoons cornstarch
1 teaspoon sesame oil
vegetable oil for stir-frying
3 teaspoons minced fresh ginger
2 large garlic cloves, chopped

1. Mix soy sauce, mirin, broth, lemon juice, rind, sugar, salt, water, cornstarch, and sesame oil in a bowl.
2. Heat wok and add oil. When hot, add half the wings and stir-fry until browned on both sides, about 5 minutes. Remove to a plate. Add remaining wings and fry until browned.
3. Add ginger and garlic and the browned wings. Lower heat slightly and cook, stirring occasionally for 25 to 30 minutes or until cooked through.
4. Stir seasoning liquid and add to wings. Turn heat to high and bring to a boil. Heat for a few seconds, stirring, until thickly glazed.
5. Transfer to a platter and serve.

Serves 2 to 4

DEEP-FRIED WINGS

Cajun
WINGS

Sometimes one must say to heck with calories and enjoy. In the case of these zesty but calorie-laden wings, it is definitely worth it. You can always diet tomorrow — right?

2½ pounds wings, trimmed and separated
1 cup flour
2 tablespoons cornstarch
2 teaspoons baking powder
1 teaspoon salt
1 cup water
2 teaspoons crushed red pepper flakes
1 teaspoon cayenne
1 teaspoon freshly ground black pepper
1 teaspoon thyme
½ teaspoon allspice
½ teaspoon mace
vegetable oil for deep-frying

1. Combine flour, cornstarch, baking powder, salt, water, and spices and herbs in a bowl. Mix well, but only to combine.
2. Dip wings in batter. It is not necessary to completely cover wings with batter, just as much as possible.
3. Heat oil to about 370°. Deep-fry wings, a few at a time, until nicely browned and crisp, about 10 to 15 minutes. Drain on a paper-towel-lined plate.
4. Transfer to a platter and serve with Louisiana Dip (see page 98).

Serves 2 to 4

Southern Fried with Gravy

WINGS

This hearty classic American dish, usually made with cut-up chicken, has been adapted to use wings instead. I might add it is better with wings — but then it may just be my biased opinion!

2½ pounds wings, trimmed and separated
1½ cups flour
¼ teaspoon salt
¼ teaspoon finely ground black pepper
¼ teaspoon thyme
¼ teaspoon oregano
¼ teaspoon cayenne
¼ teaspoon paprika
vegetable oil for deep-frying
2 tablespoons flour
2 to 2½ cups milk
¼ teaspoon salt
½ teaspoon freshly ground black pepper

1. Mix 1½ cups flour and herbs and spices on a plate and roll wings in mixture to coat evenly.
2. Heat oil in a large heavy frying pan to around 370°. Deep-fry wings, a few at a time, until browned and crisp, about 10 to 15 minutes.
3. Transfer to a paper-towel-lined plate to drain and continue until all wings are done.
4. Pour off all but 2 tablespoons of the oil, leaving all the brown bits on the bottom of frying pan; they add flavor to the gravy.
5. Add 2 tablespoons flour and mix well. Pour in milk, a little at a time, and whisk continuously until gravy comes to the boil.
6. Add salt and pepper.
7. Transfer wings to a platter and serve with a bowl of gravy. Dip wings in peppery gravy.

Serves 2 to 4

"Drumstick"

WINGS

These tiny "drumsticks," made from the upper part of the wing, make an attractive presentation when served around a small bowl of zesty dip. The light and crispy batter covering the wings is always a favorite, especially with children.

2½ pounds wings, trimmed and separated
1 cup flour
2 tablespoons cornstarch
2 teaspoons baking powder
1 teaspoon salt
1 cup water
vegetable oil for deep-frying

1. Take the meatier section of each wing (save the other section for another recipe or stock) and scrape and push the meat to the end of the bone, using a small sharp knife. You will have a mound of meat that resembles a drumstick. Continue until all wings are done. They may be done up to this point and refrigerated until needed.
2. Combine the flour, cornstarch, baking powder, salt, and water and mix well, but only to combine. Do not overmix.
3. Dip "drumsticks" into batter.
4. Heat oil to about 370°. Deep-fry wings, a few at a time, until nicely browned and cooked through, about 10 to 15 minutes.
5. Drain on paper-towel-lined plate.
6. Transfer to a platter and serve with Spicy Apricot Dip (see page 99).

Serves 2 to 4

"Drumstick" Wings and Spicy Apricot Dip

Cornmeal Fried

WINGS

*It is nice to serve these with a choice of dips —
one spicy hot, the other cool and refreshing.*

2½ pounds wings, trimmed and separated
juice of 4 large limes
1 cup flour
1 cup cornmeal
1 teaspoon salt
¼ teaspoon freshly ground black pepper
vegetable oil for deep-frying

1. Marinate wings in lime juice for 1 hour.
2. Mix flour, cornmeal, salt, and pepper and place on a piece of waxed paper.
3. Remove wings from lime juice and coat evenly in flour mixture.
4. Heat oil in a large heavy frying pan to about 370°. Deep-fry wings, a few at a time, until nicely browned and crisp, about 10 to 15 minutes. Remove and drain on a paper-towel-lined plate.
5. Transfer to a platter and serve with Mild, Medium, or Molten Dip and Horseradish Sour Cream Dip (see page 98 and page 99).

Serves 2 to 4

INTERNATIONAL WINGS

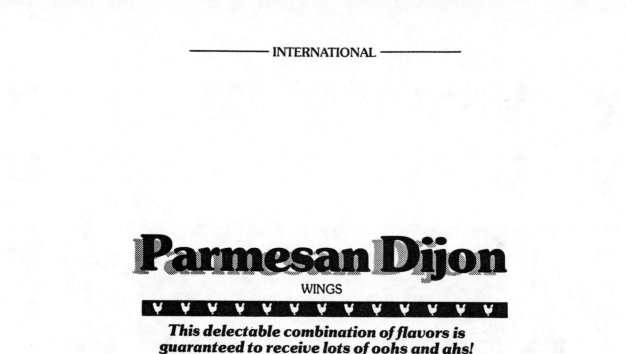

Parmesan Dijon
WINGS

This delectable combination of flavors is guaranteed to receive lots of oohs and ahs!

2½ pounds wings, trimmed and separated
½ cup (1 stick) butter
4 teaspoons Dijon-type mustard
1 large garlic clove, chopped
2 teaspoons fresh lemon juice
¼ teaspoon salt
¼ teaspoon freshly ground black pepper
¼ teaspoon oregano
¼ cup fine dry bread crumbs
¼ cup freshly grated Parmesan cheese

1. In a large heavy frying pan, melt butter over moderate heat and stir in mustard, garlic, lemon juice, salt, pepper, and oregano.
2. Add wings and fry until nicely browned on all sides, approximately 15 to 20 minutes.
3. Reduce heat and sprinkle with bread crumbs and Parmesan cheese. Toss well to coat evenly.
4. Transfer to a platter and serve.

Serves 2 to 4

Hot Red Pepper Garlic
WINGS

Without question, these are hot and utterly tasty.
If you like things lip-searing hot, by all means add
more red pepper flakes; but if you do, the other
flavors will not come through.

2½ pounds wings, trimmed and separated
½ cup (1 stick) butter, melted
2 tablespoons olive oil
2 to 3 teaspoons crushed red pepper flakes
1 small onion, chopped
4 tablespoons chopped parsley
3 large garlic cloves, chopped
¼ teaspoon salt

1. Purée basting ingredients in food processor.
2. Place wings in a large bowl, pour over puréed mixture, and stir to coat wings evenly.
3. Preheat broiler. Place wings on broiling rack and broil 15 to 20 minutes or until browned and cooked through. Turn after 10 minutes and baste with marinade.
4. Transfer to a platter and serve.

Serves 2 to 4

40 Garlic

WINGS

Anyone passionate about garlic will find these wings heaven, although you do not have to love garlic to appreciate this dish. Forty garlic cloves may sound atrocious, but in this instance the garlic is left whole and baked with olive oil and herbs, which turns the garlic from a seasoning into a tender vegetable — buttery soft and very sweet-flavored.

2½ pounds wings, trimmed and separated
½ cup olive oil
40 large garlic cloves, peeled
¼ teaspoon salt
¼ teaspoon freshly ground black pepper
¼ teaspoon rosemary
¼ teaspoon thyme
¼ teaspoon oregano
1 tablespoon Pernod
French bread

1. Preheat oven to 425°.
2. Place wings and remaining ingredients in a large casserole and toss to distribute garlic cloves and seasonings around wings.
3. Cover casserole and bake for 1 hour or until garlic cloves are tender.
4. Transfer wings to a platter and serve with crusty bread to dip in the garlicky oil. The garlic cloves may be eaten as they are or spread on the bread.

Serves 2 to 4

Curried

WINGS

These popular wings are braised in a mellow curry sauce — no hot spices in this curry. Definitely serve rice with this dish.

2½ pounds wings, trimmed and separated
7 tablespoons butter
2 tablespoons flour
2 tablespoons curry powder, or more to taste
1 medium onion, finely chopped
1 large garlic clove, chopped
½ green pepper, chopped
2 large ripe tomatoes, chopped
1 bay leaf
½ teaspoon salt
¼ teaspoon freshly ground black pepper
1 tablespoon lemon juice
1 teaspoon grated lemon rind
1 cup chicken broth
3 tablespoons dry white vermouth
2 tablespoons raisins

1. Melt butter in a large frying pan and fry wings, a few at a time, until browned on both sides. Remove to a plate. Blend flour and curry powder in butter.
2. Add onion, garlic, green pepper, tomatoes, bay leaf, salt, pepper, lemon juice, and lemon rind. Heat and stir for a few minutes.
3. Add broth and vermouth. Stir to blend.
4. Add browned wings and cover. Cook 35 to 40 minutes or until wings are very tender, lifting lid and stirring occasionally. During the last 10 minutes add raisins.
5. Transfer to a platter and serve.

Serves 2 to 4

Goat Cheese
WINGS

These trendy wings are quite rich to serve on their own. I suggest you serve them with other wings, such as Drunken Wings or Hot Red Pepper Garlic Wings.

2½ pounds wings, trimmed and separated
6 ounces fresh, mild goat cheese
3 tablespoons butter, at room temperature
4 tablespoons chopped parsley
1 whole medium green onion, chopped
¼ teaspoon thyme
¼ teaspoon oregano
⅛ teaspoon salt
¼ teaspoon freshly ground black pepper
1 teaspoon Worcestershire sauce
1 teaspoon Tabasco sauce
1 cup fine dry bread crumbs

1. Preheat oven to 400°.
2. Purée everything except bread crumbs (and wings of course!) in a food processor until smooth.
3. Coat wings with goat cheese mixture by spreading it on with your fingers.
4. Put bread crumbs on a plate and roll goat-cheese-covered wings in crumbs.
5. Place in a large baking pan and bake 30 to 45 minutes, turning once or twice, until nicely browned and cooked through.
6. Transfer to a platter and serve.

Serves 2 to 4

Hot and Spicy
WINGS

Here are nice spicy wings that are also excellent served at room temperature, making them perfect for picnics or casual lunches.

2½ pounds wings, trimmed and separated
½ cup (1 stick) butter
4 tablespoons Dijon-type mustard
1 large garlic clove, chopped
1 tablespoon fresh lime juice
3 teaspoons sambal oelek or Tabasco sauce
½ cup fine dry bread crumbs

1. In a large heavy frying pan, melt butter over moderate heat and stir in mustard, garlic, lime juice, and sambal oelek.
2. Add wings and fry until nicely browned on all sides, approximately 20 to 25 minutes.
3. Reduce heat and sprinkle with bread crumbs. Toss well to coat evenly.
4. Transfer to a platter and serve.

Serves 2 to 4

*These are best served at room temperature.

747's – Smoky Turkey
WINGS

My husband Drew thought it would be fun to have a recipe for jumbo wings and so he named them 747's. They have a subtle smoked flavor that is best served at room temperature.

2 pounds turkey wings, trimmed and separated
4 cups cold water
2 large garlic cloves, crushed
1 tablespoon salt
1 teaspoon freshly ground black pepper
⅓ cup mild honey
½ teaspoon liquid smoke
5 teaspoons peanut oil
1 teaspoon liquid smoke

1. Combine water, garlic, salt, pepper, honey, and ½ teaspoon liquid smoke in a bowl large enough to accommodate turkey wings.
2. Add wings, stir, and marinate for 2 hours at room temperature. Stir wings occasionally. Drain and discard marinade.
3. Preheat oven to 400°. Mix 5 teaspoons oil with 1 teaspoon liquid smoke and brush wings lightly with this mixture. Place on broiling rack and roast for 1 hour or until done. Brush wings every 15 minutes with liquid smoke mixture.
4. Remove from oven and cool. To allow subtle smoke flavor to come through, serve at room temperature.

Serves 2

*These are best served at room temperature.

Lemon Honey
WINGS

This combination of lemon, honey, and spices makes delicious wings.

2½ pounds wings, trimmed and separated
grated rind of 2 medium lemons
juice of 2 medium lemons
3 tablespoons mild honey
1 tablespoon olive oil
2 large garlic cloves, chopped
½ teaspoon ground cumin
½ teaspoon ground coriander
¼ teaspoon salt
¼ teaspoon freshly ground black pepper

1. Mix marinade ingredients in a bowl large enough to hold wings. Add wings, stir, and marinate for 2 hours at room temperature. Drain and reserve marinade.
2. Preheat broiler. Place wings on broiling rack and broil 15 to 20 minutes or until browned. Turn after 10 minutes and baste with marinade.
3. Transfer to a platter and serve.

Serves 2 to 4

Herb

WINGS

The seasoning here is classic Tuscan, the flavor is divine.

2½ pounds wings, trimmed and separated
¼ cup dry white wine
⅓ cup olive oil
grated rind of 2 medium lemons
juice of 2 medium lemons
2 large garlic cloves, chopped
4 tablespoons minced parsley
1 teaspoon oregano
1 teaspoon thyme
¼ teaspoon salt
¼ teaspoon freshly ground black pepper

1. Mix marinade ingredients in a bowl large enough to accommodate wings. Add wings, stir, and marinate for 2 hours at room temperature. Drain and reserve marinade.
2. Preheat broiler. Place wings on broiling rack and broil 15 to 20 minutes or until browned and cooked through. Turn after 10 minutes and baste with marinade.
3. Transfer to a platter and serve.

Serves 2 to 4

Smoke and Spice

WINGS

The secret ingredient in these spicy and offbeat wings is liquid smoke.

2½ pounds wings, trimmed and separated
4 tablespoons olive oil
2 medium onions, chopped
5 to 6 large garlic cloves, chopped
1 can (28 ounces) tomatoes
1 can (5½ ounces) tomato paste
2 tablespoons sugar
2 tablespoons red wine vinegar
2 tablespoons Worcestershire sauce
1 tablespoon liquid smoke
1 teaspoon salt
1 teaspoon oregano
1 teaspoon cinnamon
1 tablespoon dry mustard
4 tablespoons butter

1. Heat olive oil in a heavy noncorrosive saucepan and sauté onions and garlic until soft but not brown. Add everything except wings, stir, and cook uncovered over medium heat for ½ hour or until thickened enough to coat a spoon. Cool.
2. Place wings in a large bowl and pour cooled marinade over wings. Stir to coat well and marinate for 2 hours at room temperature. Drain and reserve marinade.
3. Preheat broiler. Place wings on broiling rack and broil 15 to 20 minutes or until browned and cooked through. Turn after 10 minutes and baste with marinade.
4. Transfer to a platter and serve.

Serves 2 to 4

Pecan Orange
WINGS

These simple but fancy wings are sweet and nutty-tasting with a hint of orange.

2½ pounds wings, trimmed and separated
grated rind of 1 large orange
½ cup orange juice, fresh or frozen
2 tablespoons Cointreau or Grand Marnier
¼ cup olive oil
2 tablespoons mild honey
¼ cup pecans, very finely chopped
⅛ teaspoon ground cloves
pinch of dry mustard

1. Mix marinade ingredients in a bowl large enough to hold wings. Add wings, stir, and marinate for 2 hours at room temperature. Drain and reserve marinade.
2. Preheat broiler. Place wings on broiling rack and broil 15 to 20 minutes or until browned and cooked through. Turn after 10 minutes and baste with marinade.
3. When wings are almost done, pour remaining marinade into saucepan and boil on high heat until reduced slightly.
4. Transfer wings to a platter and serve with hot marinade as a dipping sauce.

Serves 2 to 4

Pan-Fried Garlicky

WINGS

*This version of garlic and wings is very rustic —
meaning oily and garlicky. It is quite good, but
only to those who love olive oil and garlic in
abundance.*

2½ pounds wings, trimmed and separated
¼ cup olive oil
10 large garlic cloves, lightly crushed
¼ teaspoon salt
¼ teaspoon freshly ground black pepper

1. Heat olive oil in a large frying pan. Add wings and remaining ingredients and fry until wings are nicely browned and cooked through, around 25 to 30 minutes. Do not burn garlic cloves or they will be bitter.
2. Transfer to a platter with sauce and garlic cloves spooned on top.

Serves 2 to 4

Moroccan
WINGS

An incredibly aromatic marinade that produces
gloriously flavorful and spicy wings.

2½ pounds wings, trimmed and separated
6 tablespoons olive oil
juice of 2 medium lemons
2 large garlic cloves, chopped
1 small onion, minced
4 tablespoons minced parsley
1 tablespoon coriander seeds, crushed finely
3 teaspoons sambal oelek or Tabasco sauce
2 teaspoons ground cumin

1. Mix marinade ingredients in a bowl large enough to hold wings. Add wings, stir, and marinate for 2 hours at room temperature. Drain and reserve marinade.
2. Preheat broiler. Place wings on broiling rack and broil 15 to 20 minutes or until browned and cooked through. Turn after 10 minutes and baste with marinade.
3. Transfer to a platter and serve.

Serves 2 to 4

Moroccan Wings, Creamy Cole Slaw, and Maple Ginger Beans

Deviled
WINGS

This marinade produces nice crispy wings with absolutely terrific flavor.

2½ pounds wings, trimmed and separated
4 large garlic cloves, chopped
4 tablespoons soy sauce
2 tablespoons olive oil
4 tablespoons Dijon-type mustard
1 cup fine dry bread crumbs
¼ teaspoon salt
¼ teaspoon freshly ground black pepper

1. Mix garlic, soy sauce, olive oil, and mustard in a bowl large enough to accommodate wings.
2. Add wings and stir to coat evenly. Add bread crumbs, salt, and pepper and stir again to coat wings with crumbs.
3. Preheat broiler. Place wings on broiling rack and broil 15 to 20 minutes or until browned and cooked through.
4. Transfer to a platter and serve.

Serves 2 to 4

Hot Pepper Jelly
WINGS

For these wings you will have to make your own hot pepper jelly or buy a jar in a specialty food shop. Recipes for hot pepper jelly can be found in a few Tex-Mex, American Southwest, or preserving cookbooks.

2½ pounds wings, trimmed and separated
½ cup hot pepper jelly
grated rind of 1 large orange
⅛ cup orange juice, fresh or frozen
2 large garlic cloves, chopped
4 tablespoons olive oil

1. Mix marinade ingredients in a bowl large enough to accommodate wings. Add wings, stir, and marinate for 2 hours at room temperature. Drain and reserve marinade.
2. Preheat broiler. Place wings on broiling rack and broil 15 to 20 minutes or until browned and cooked through. Turn after 10 minutes and baste with marinade.
3. Transfer to a platter and serve.

Serves 2 to 4

Maple Syrup
WINGS

*Use only 100 percent maple syrup for these
sweetly glazed wings. They tend to brown easily,
so watch them carefully.*

2½ pounds wings, trimmed and separated
¼ cup Bold 'n Spicy or Dijon-type mustard
1 cup water
½ cup ketchup
½ cup pure maple syrup
¼ cup rice vinegar
1 small onion, minced
1 teaspoon sambal oelek or Tabasco sauce
1 tablespoon Worcestershire sauce
1 teaspoon salt
¼ teaspoon freshly ground black pepper

**1. Mix marinade ingredients in a bowl large
enough to accommodate wings. Add
wings, stir, and marinate for 2 hours at
room temperature. Drain and reserve
marinade.**
**2. Preheat broiler. Place wings on broiling
rack and broil 15 to 20 minutes or until
browned and cooked through. Turn after
10 minutes and baste with marinade.**
3. Transfer to a platter and serve.

Serves 2 to 4

Greek

WINGS

Thyme is rarely used in Greek cooking except when mixed with olives preserved in oil. But here it adds an interesting touch to traditional Greek seasonings.

2½ pounds wings, trimmed and separated
4 tablespoons olive oil
4 tablespoons fresh lemon juice
2 large garlic cloves, chopped
1 teaspoon salt
½ teaspoon oregano
1 teaspoon thyme
1 teaspoon freshly ground black pepper

1. Mix marinade ingredients in a large bowl. Add wings, stir, and marinate for 2 hours at room temperature. Drain and reserve marinade.
2. Preheat broiler. Place wings on broiling rack and broil 15 to 20 minutes or until browned and cooked through. Turn after 10 minutes and baste with marinade.
3. Transfer to a platter and serve.

Serves 2 to 4

Pickled

WINGS

Pickling spices are usually a blend of aromatic spices and peppers and are available in the spice department at supermarkets. Yes, these wings are truly unusual and only for the adventurous palate. If you enjoy giving your taste buds something different now and then, by all means try these amusing wings.

2½ pounds wings, trimmed and separated
4 large garlic cloves, chopped
¼ teaspoon salt
¼ teaspoon freshly ground black pepper
1½ tablespoons pickling spices
2 tablespoons red wine vinegar
4 tablespoons olive oil
3 tablespoons water
juice of 1 lemon

1. Mix marinade ingredients in a bowl large enough to accommodate wings. Add wings, stir, and marinate for 2 hours at room temperature. Drain and reserve marinade.
2. Preheat broiler. Place wings on broiling rack and broil 15 to 20 minutes or until browned and cooked through. Turn after 10 minutes and baste with marinade.
3. Transfer to a platter and serve.

Serves 2 to 4

Tandoori

WINGS

Tandoori is an Indian method of cooking in a tandoor (a clay-lined pit oven), which bakes, barbecues, and roasts meat simultaneously. This process can be adequately duplicated in a broiler or on a barbecue and, using the correct seasonings, produces beautifully colored and moist wings.

2½ pounds wings, trimmed and separated
1 cup plain yogurt
2 tablespoons minced fresh ginger
4 large garlic cloves, chopped
1 teaspoon curry powder
¼ teaspoon turmeric
½ teaspoon ground cumin
½ teaspoon dry mustard
1 teaspoon crushed red pepper flakes
1 teaspoon salt
½ teaspoon freshly ground black pepper
juice of ½ large lemon
2 tablespoons vegetable oil

1. Blend marinade ingredients in a large bowl. Add wings, stir well, and marinate for 2 hours at room temperature. Drain and reserve marinade.
2. Preheat broiler. Place wings on broiling rack and broil 15 to 20 minutes or until browned and cooked through. Turn after 10 minutes and baste with marinade.
3. Transfer to a platter and serve.

Serves 2 to 4

Cinnamon Honey
WINGS

The following marinade creates unique-tasting wings with just a hint of cinnamon.

2½ pounds wings, trimmed and separated
4 large garlic cloves, chopped
¼ cup olive oil
2 tablespoons soy sauce
¼ cup rice vinegar
¼ cup mild honey
1½ teaspoons cinnamon
1 teaspoon thyme
½ teaspoon ground ginger
½ teaspoon dry mustard

1. Mix marinade ingredients in a large bowl. Add wings, stir, and marinate for 2 hours at room temperature. Drain and reserve marinade.
2. Preheat broiler. Place wings on broiling rack and broil until cooked through and nicely browned, approximately 15 to 20 minutes. Turn after 10 minutes and baste with marinade.
3. Transfer to a platter and serve.

Serves 2 to 4

Mexican Mole Sauce

WINGS

Wings for Mexican food aficionados. The national dish of Mexico is Turkey in Mole (pronounced mo-lay) Sauce. This festive dish has been adapted for wings. Do not let the chocolate inhibit you from trying this classic sauce. It is hot and spicy and very, very unusual.

2½ pounds wings, trimmed and separated
4 large garlic cloves, peeled
1 medium onion, roughly chopped
4 teaspoons sambal oelek
1 tablespoon sesame seeds
½ corn tortilla, torn into pieces
1 tablespoon raisins
¼ teaspoon ground cloves
¼ teaspoon ground coriander seeds
¼ teaspoon cinnamon
¼ teaspoon salt
¼ teaspoon freshly ground black pepper
vegetable oil for sautéing and deep-frying
1 ounce unsweetened chocolate, grated
2 teaspoons sugar
1 can (28 ounces) tomatoes, drained
1 cup chicken broth
sesame seeds for garnish

1. Purée garlic, onion, sambal oelek, 1 tablespoon sesame seeds, tortilla pieces, raisins, cloves, coriander seeds, cinnamon, salt, and pepper in food processor until smooth.
2. Sauté the puréed mixture in oil in a heavy noncorrosive saucepan for 10 minutes, stirring constantly.
3. Add grated chocolate and sugar and stir until melted.
4. Add tomatoes and broth and simmer sauce for 45 minutes to 1 hour or until as thick as tomato sauce. Stir constantly and watch that it does not burn.
5. Heat oil to 370° in a heavy large frying pan. Deep-fry wings for 10 to 15 minutes or until cooked and crisp, in two batches if necessary, and remove to a paper-towel-lined plate to drain.
6. Place wings in saucepan with mole sauce. Heat and mix well for 5 minutes.
7. Transfer to a platter. Sprinkle with sesame seeds and serve.

Serves 2 to 4

Honey Curry
WINGS

*The pairing of honey and curry gives these wings
their spectacular flavor.*

2½ pounds wings, trimmed and separated
¼ cup olive oil
4 teaspoons curry powder
2 large garlic cloves, chopped
4 tablespoons mild honey
¼ teaspoon salt

1. Mix marinade ingredients in a bowl large enough to hold wings. Add wings, stir, and marinate for 2 hours at room temperature. Drain and reserve marinade.
2. Preheat broiler. Place wings on broiling rack and broil 15 to 20 minutes or until browned and cooked through. Turn after 10 minutes and baste with marinade.
3. Transfer to a platter and serve.

Serves 2 to 4

SIDE ORDERS

Maple Ginger Beans

These terrific beans receive raves every time they are served. They are hot and spicy and unbelievably quick to cook; yet they taste as if they have been slow-baked for hours.

2 tablespoons butter
2 large garlic cloves, chopped
1 medium onion, minced
1 can (19 ounces) white kidney beans, drained and rinsed
¼ cup 100 percent maple syrup
⅛ cup Durkee Red Hot sauce
⅛ cup ketchup
¼ teaspoon ground cloves
¼ teaspoon ground ginger
1 teaspoon salt
1 teaspoon dry mustard

1. Melt butter in a heavy saucepan and cook garlic and onion until soft but not browned.
2. Add remaining ingredients, stir, and bring to a boil.
3. Reduce heat to just simmering, cover, and cook 20 to 25 minutes or until thickened, lifting lid and stirring beans occasionally. Serve immediately.

Serves 4

Herb Buttered Corn

If you have only tasted corn with butter and salt, try this herb butter next time. The herbs and seasonings enhance the corn's flavor tremendously.

¼ cup (½ stick) butter
2 tablespoons minced parsley
1 whole small green onion, chopped
1½ tablespoons fresh lemon juice
¾ teaspoon salt
½ teaspoon freshly ground black pepper
½ teaspoon Tabasco sauce
1 teaspoon Worcestershire sauce
6 ears of corn

1. Purée ingredients in food processor and place in small serving dish.
2. Leave at room temperature if using within a ½ hour or refrigerate covered and remove ½ hour before serving.
3. Remove corn husks and silk and discard.
4. Bring a large pot of water to a full rolling boil. Add corn and cook for 8 minutes. Drain.
5. Serve corn with herb butter on the side.

Makes enough butter for 6 ears of corn

Deep-Fried Potato Skins

These are what potato chips are supposed to taste like—fresh and delicious. Since you are only using the potato skins for this recipe, save the potatoes for use in another dish.

6 large baking potatoes
vegetable oil for deep-frying
salt

1. Scrub potatoes and dry well with paper towels.
2. Cut potato skins into 3-by-1½-inch strips with a sharp knife. Each strip should have some potato attached to the skin.
3. Heat oil to 370°. Deep-fry potato skins, a few at a time, for about 5 minutes, or until crisp and light brown.
4. Remove to drain on a paper-towel-lined plate and sprinkle with salt.
5. Serve immediately.

Serves 4

French-Fried Mushrooms

*I have turned more mushroom haters into
mushroom lovers with this recipe. It is a fun side
dish and also makes a great appetizer or late-
night snack. It is imperative that you serve them
with Horseradish Sour Cream Dip because this
dip complements the mushrooms perfectly.*

1 pound whole mushrooms, wiped clean
1 egg, well beaten
½ cup milk
½ teaspoon salt
⅓ cup flour
1 cup fine dry bread crumbs
vegetable oil for deep-frying

1. Beat egg with milk and salt.
2. Place flour on a piece of waxed paper
and the bread crumbs on another piece of
waxed paper.
3. Roll mushrooms in flour. Dip them one
at a time in egg mixture and then in bread
crumbs. Be sure they are evenly coated.
4. Heat oil to 370°. When hot, add only as
many mushrooms as will fit without
overcrowding, and cook about 5 minutes,
or until golden brown.
5. Remove and drain on paper-towel-lined
plate. Continue until all are done.
6. Sprinkle immediately with salt and serve
hot with Horseradish Sour Cream Dip
(see page 99).

Serves 2 to 4

Deep-Fried Onion Rings

Crisp-fried onion rings are always a hit with kids.

2 medium onions, very thinly sliced
1 cup flour
2 tablespoons cornstarch
2 teaspoons baking powder
1 teaspoon salt
1 cup water
vegetable oil for deep-frying

1. Combine flour, cornstarch, baking powder, salt, and water and mix well, but only to combine.
2. Heat oil to 370°. Separate onion slices into rings and dip into batter. Add to oil, a few at a time, and fry until crisp and golden, about 5 minutes.
3. Remove and drain on a paper-towel-lined plate. Continue until all are done.
4. Serve immediately.

Serves 4

SALADS

Creamy Cole Slaw

Instead of shredding the vegetables by hand, you may shred the cored cabbage and vegetables in a food processor (using the proper disk for shredding), then put the knife blade in place and chop the onions. You may then add the remaining ingredients to the food processor all at once and turn it on a few times to mix well. Cole Slaw tends to exude a lot of liquid. Drain the salad before serving if necessary.

1 pound cabbage, cored and shredded
2 medium carrots, shredded
1 medium sweet red pepper, shredded
1 small green pepper, shredded
1 medium onion, finely chopped
2 tablespoons red wine vinegar
2 teaspoons sugar
½ teaspoon salt
½ teaspoon freshly ground black pepper
1 cup homemade or Hellman's mayonnaise
2 tablespoons heavy cream
2 teaspoons caraway seeds

1. Mix ingredients well in a large bowl (or make in food processor), cover, and refrigerate several hours before serving. Stir well again before serving.

Serves 4 to 6

Old-Fashioned Potato Salad

♥ ♥ ♥ ♥ ♥ ♥ ♥ ♥ ♥ ♥ ♥

This is potato salad like the kind you wish your mother had made! Absolutely every person who tastes it always says it is the best potato salad they have ever had — and by the way, it goes with pretty well every recipe in the book, including the Oriental recipes.

9 to 10 medium potatoes
3 tablespoons vinegar
½ cup potato water
2½ teaspoons salt
¾ teaspoon freshly ground black pepper
1 medium onion, finely chopped
1 medium celery stalk, finely minced
3 hard-boiled eggs, very finely minced
½ cup minced parsley
¾ cup homemade or Hellman's mayonnaise

1. Scrub unpeeled potatoes and boil until tender but not mushy (or too firm either). Drain, reserving ½ cup potato water.
2. Allow potatoes to cool only enough to handle them, then peel.
3. Cut into ½-inch squares and put in a large bowl. Mix vinegar with potato water and pour over potatoes. Add salt and pepper. Stir well but gently.
4. Add everything except the mayonnaise and mix well. Place bowl in freezer, about 3 to 5 minutes, or just long enough to chill ingredients quickly. Remove and add mayonnaise.
5. Stir and correct seasonings, if necessary, and refrigerate at least several hours or overnight before serving.

Serves 6

Tarragon Macaroni Salad

Most macaroni salads are quite mundane. Not this one! It is stylish and elegant, the tarragon adding the sophisticated touch. Although you may substitute a green pepper for the sweet red pepper called for, the flavor will not be as exquisite.

2 cups elbow macaroni, cooked, drained, and rinsed in cold water to cool
1 medium celery stalk, minced
1 small onion, minced
1 large sweet red pepper, chopped into ½-inch pieces
⅔ cup homemade or Hellman's mayonnaise
2 tablespoons rice vinegar
1½ teaspoons salt
¼ teaspoon freshly ground black pepper
2 teaspoons tarragon

1. Mix ingredients, cover, and chill for several hours before serving.

Serves 4 to 6

Creamy Garlic Dressing

The lowly iceberg lettuce is brought to life with this garlicky dressing. Its watery, crunchy qualities go well with the creamy topping. You may serve this on other greens as well.

½ teaspoon salt
1 teaspoon Canadian whisky
3 tablespoons tomato paste
3 to 4 large garlic cloves, minced
½ pint heavy cream
2 large wedges of iceberg lettuce

1. **Whisk dressing ingredients until well blended.**
2. **Chill several hours.**
3. **Serve on wedges of iceberg lettuce.**

Serves 2

Cucumber Sour Cream Salad

Here is a simple, refreshing salad that should be served well chilled. This goes very well with almost every wing dish, particularly those that are broiled or barbecued.

2 medium cucumbers, peeled and thinly sliced
2 medium onions, thinly sliced
2 cups sour cream
3 tablespoons white vinegar
1 teaspoon salt
¾ teaspoon freshly ground black pepper

1. Toss vegetables and dressing in bowl.
2. Chill for at least 2 hours in refrigerator before serving.

Serves 2 to 4

DIPPING SAUCES

Mild, Medium, or Molten Dip

The ingredients below are for Molten Dip. To make Mild or Medium, just reduce the amount of pepper and Worcestershire sauce to taste. This dip, served along with Horseradish Sour Cream Dip, is excellent with Crispy Breaded Wings.

½ cup ketchup
1 teaspoon freshly ground black pepper
1 ounce Canadian whisky
1 long dash Worcestershire sauce
1 medium garlic clove, finely chopped
1 tablespoon tomato paste
2 tablespoons red wine vinegar

1. Combine ingredients in a small bowl.
2. Serve with deep-fried wings.

Makes approximately ¾ cup

Louisiana Dip

This is excellent for dipping Cajun Wings.

¼ cup Durkee Red Hot sauce
¼ cup (½ stick) butter

1. Melt butter slowly and do not brown. Add Durkee Red Hot sauce, mix, and pour into a small serving bowl.

Makes approximately ½ cup

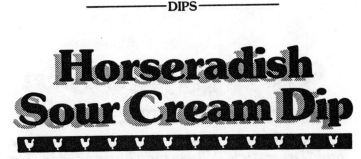

Horseradish Sour Cream Dip

Anything deep-fried, such as Crispy Breaded Wings, Cornmeal Fried Wings, or French-Fried Mushrooms, is heavenly with this dip.

3 tablespoons bottled horseradish
1 cup sour cream

1. Mix well, chill, and serve in a small bowl.

Makes approximately 1 cup

Spicy Apricot Dip

Serve this with "Drumstick" Wings.

¼ cup apricot jam
½ cup rice vinegar
3 tablespoons water
½ teaspoon Durkee Red Hot sauce or
Tabasco sauce

1. Purée in food processor.
2. Pour into small serving bowl and serve.

Makes approximately ¾ cup

Soy Honey Dip

Crispy Breaded Wings, Cornmeal Fried Wings, and "Drumstick" Wings may be dunked in this sweet dip.

2 teaspoons soy sauce
⅛ cup mild honey

1. Mix ingredients in a small bowl and serve.

Makes approximately ⅛ cup

Soy Lemon Dip

You may dip any of the following wings in this dip: Crispy Breaded Wings, Cornmeal Fried Wings, Cajun Wings, Thai Stuffed Wings, or "Drumstick" Wings.

1 medium garlic clove, minced
grated rind of 1 lemon
juice of 1 lemon
¼ cup soy sauce
4 teaspoons mild honey
1 teaspoon sesame oil
2 teaspoons Durkee Red Hot sauce or
Tabasco sauce

1. Mix ingredients in a small bowl and serve.

Makes approximately ½ cup

MORE WINGS

The Ultimate

WINGS

This is a recipe I developed for a Crisco oil advertising campaign. The objective was to create Buffalo style wings with a sauce that would cling and be absorbed into the wing, making a "drier," more intensely flavored wing — as opposed to my "wetter" original recipe on page 22. The secret I discovered was to double-fry the wings; first in Crisco oil, then in the sauce. This is now my favorite way to cook them. Try them, they are the ultimate!

2 pounds wings, trimmed and separated Buffalo-style
2 cups Crisco oil
¼ cup Durkee Red Hot sauce
1 tablespoon Crisco oil
1 teaspoon butter
1 teaspoon cider vinegar
¼ teaspoon garlic powder
1 tablespoon or more ketchup (optional)

1. In medium nonstick skillet, heat 2 cups oil to 375°. Deep-fry wings 8 to 10 minutes or until nicely browned and crisp.
2. Meanwhile, combine hot sauce, 1 tablespoon oil, butter, vinegar, and garlic powder in a small bowl. Add 1 to 3 tablespoons ketchup if you prefer a milder sauce.
3. With tongs, remove browned wings to a paper-towel-lined plate. Pour oil into a heatproof bowl and immediately place skillet back on an *unheated* element. Pour sauce into skillet; add wings and gently toss

30 seconds. Place skillet back on the heated element (medium heat). Continue tossing 2 minutes or until wings have completely absorbed sauce. Serve at once.

Serves 2

BLUE CHEESE DRESSING
1 large egg
2 tablespoons red wine vinegar
2 tablespoons Dijon-type mustard
salt and pepper
1 cup Crisco oil
4 tablespoons blue cheese
celery or carrot sticks

1. In blender or food processor, combine egg, vinegar, mustard, and salt and pepper. With machine running, pour in oil in thin stream. Stop machine. Add blue cheese, then combine until smooth. Taste for seasoning. Serve with celery or carrot sticks.

Makes about 1¼ cups.

Triple Mustard
WINGS

*Although marinated in three types of mustard,
there is only a subtle, sweet hint of it
in these yummy wings.*

2½ pounds wings, trimmed and separated
¼ cup Dijon-type mustard
¼ cup prepared Russian-style sweet mustard
1 teaspoon dry mustard
1 tablespoon olive oil
2 teaspoons red wine vinegar
¼ teaspoon cayenne
¼ teaspoon freshly ground black pepper
½ cup dry bread crumbs
½ cup freshly grated Parmesan cheese

1. Combine mustards, oil, vinegar, cayenne, and pepper in a large bowl. Add wings and toss to coat evenly. Marinate for 1 to 2 hours at room temperature.
2. Combine bread crumbs and cheese in another bowl and coat wings with crumb mixture.
3. Preheat broiler. Place wings on a well-oiled broiling rack and broil 15 to 20 minutes (no need to turn) or until browned and cooked through. Transfer to a platter and serve.

Serves 2 to 4

Caribbean
WINGS

*Intriguingly spiced. But if you prefer your wings
hotter and spicier (I do!), just add more
paprika, pepper, and hot sauce to taste.*

2½ pounds wings, trimmed and separated
juice of 1 large lime
4 large garlic cloves, minced
3 teaspoons paprika
2 teaspoons freshly ground black pepper
⅛ teaspoon salt
1 teaspoon Tabasco sauce
1 teaspoon soy sauce
1 cup flour
oil for deep-frying

1. In a large bowl, toss wings with lime juice.
Add seasonings (not flour or oil), one at a
time, tossing wings to coat each time before
adding next ingredient.
2. Dip wings in flour to coat evenly.
3. Heat oil in a large heavy frying pan to
about 370°. Deep-fry wings 10 minutes or
until browned and crisp. Drain on a paper-
towel-lined plate and serve.

Serves 2 to 4

Horseradish

WINGS

*Believe it or not, this unlikely marinade —
basically a shrimp cocktail sauce —
produces superb tangy wings!*

2½ pounds wings, trimmed and separated
juice of 1 large lemon
½ cup ketchup
5 tablespoons prepared horseradish
3 tablespoons olive oil
1 tablespoon Worcestershire sauce
½ teaspoon Tabasco sauce
½ teaspoon freshly ground black pepper

1. Mix marinade ingredients in a bowl large enough to accommodate wings. Add wings, stir, and marinate for 2 hours at room temperature. Drain and reserve marinade.
2. Preheat broiler. Place wings on broiling rack, spoon over some marinade, and broil 15 to 20 minutes or until cooked through. Turn after 10 minutes and baste with marinade.
3. Transfer to a platter and serve.

Serves 2 to 4

Orange Marmalade
WINGS

*For this recipe, I use thick-cut Seville orange marmalade
for a delightful bittersweet taste.*

2½ pounds wings, trimmed and separated
¼ cup flour
½ cup dry bread crumbs
1 tablespoon paprika
1 tablespoon oregano
¼ teaspoon salt
½ teaspoon freshly ground black pepper
¼ cup oil for frying
2 large garlic cloves, finely chopped
½ cup orange marmalade
½ cup fresh orange juice

1. Combine flour, bread crumbs, paprika, oregano, salt and pepper in a large bowl. Dip wings in flour mixture to coat evenly.
2. Heat oil in a large heavy frying pan. Add garlic and cook 2 minutes. Add wings and cook 5 minutes, or until browned on both sides.
3. Pour off oil.
4. In a small bowl, combine marmalade and orange juice and pour over wings. Bring to a boil on medium heat, reduce heat to simmer, and cook, stirring gently, until thickly glazed, about 10 minutes.
5. Transfer to a platter and serve.

Serves 2 to 4

Five Spice

WINGS

Similar to **Chinese Barbecued Wings** *on page 48 but without the hoisin sauce, the flavor of five spice powder is more pronounced. You must use excellent-quality five spice powder — many taste too harsh — for best results. Keep trying different brands until you find one you like.*

2½ pounds wings, trimmed and separated
¼ cup soy sauce
¼ cup dry sherry
⅓ cup ketchup
⅓ cup brown sugar
¼ inch-piece fresh ginger, grated
4 large garlic cloves, finely chopped
½ teaspoon five spice powder
¼ teaspoon Tabasco sauce
2 tablespoons peanut oil

1. Mix marinade ingredients in a large bowl. Add wings, stir, and marinate for 2 hours at room temperature. Drain and reserve marinade.
2. Preheat broiler. Place wings on broiling rack and spoon over some marinade. Broil 15 to 20 minutes or until browned and cooked through. Turn after 10 minutes and baste with marinade.
3. Transfer to a platter and serve.

Serves 2 to 4

Sticky
WINGS

Sweet and sticky. Kids adore 'em.
Be sure to have plenty of napkins and finger bowls on hand!

2½ pounds wings, trimmed and separated
3 tablespoons soy sauce
2½ tablespoons dry sherry
4 tablespoons honey
1 teaspoon sambel oelek (optional)

1. Place glaze ingredients only in a heavy saucepan large enough to accommodate wings. Stir to mix.
2. Add wings and toss to coat.
3. Bring to a boil, reduce heat to a low simmer, cover, and cook for 10 minutes, stirring occasionally.
4. Remove lid and turn heat to medium. Stir and cook wings for 10 minutes, or until wings are nicely glazed and there is no sauce left.
5. Transfer to a platter and serve hot.

Serves 2 to 4

Index

ABOUT THE AUTHOR

Joie Warner is a food journalist, recipe developer, and author of several cookbooks including, *All the Best Pasta Sauces*; *All the Best Salads*; *All the Best Pizzas*; *All the Best Mexican Meals*; *All the Best Muffins and Quick Breads*; *All the Best Chicken Dinners*; *All the Best Stir-Fries*; *All the Best Potatoes*; *All the Best Cookies*; *All the Best Rice*; *All the Best Pasta Sauces II*; *The Complete Book of Chicken Wings*; *The Braun Hand Blender Cookbook*; *A Taste of Chinatown*; *Joie Warner's Spaghetti*; *Joie Warner's Caesar Salads*; and *Joie Warner's Apple Desserts*.